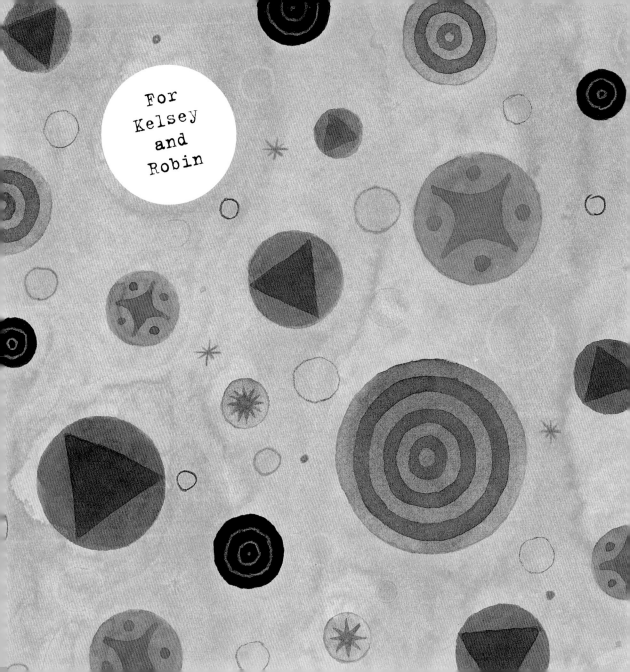

For
Kelsey
and
Robin

My Friend Chicken

by Adam McCauley

chronicle books · san francisco

From W + F AM interns   May 2001

Connie

kiyomia

Maria

Mary Ann

If thunder rrrumbled
and lightning crack-acked
If the sky rained down
pink lemonade...

If rockets rrroared by
  and fish flew through the sky
    If a polka dot bus drove through town....

I wouldn't notice!

If giraffes danced the tango
across my bedroom rug
    and the walls became
mulberry trees...

I'd pay no attention!

Why?
Because all I can think about
is my friend Chicken.

Chicken, my friend,
    I miss him so much!
Where, oh where
        did he go?

Did he fly off
    to visit the moon?

Did he paddle a canoe
down the Amazon?

Did he move to the city
and become an opera star?

Chicken, my friend,
  wherever you are
please come back home soon!

Nothing is as fun
  without you here.

My teeter won't totter.

My merry won't go round.

Rollercoasters
are a bore.

Fireworks
make me snore.

Badminton
  just makes me sad.

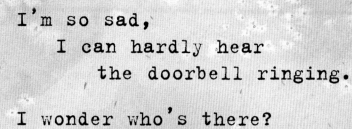

I'm so sad,
  I can hardly hear
    the doorbell ringing.

I wonder who's there?
  Could it be...

My friend Chicken!

Book design by Cynthia Wigginton.
Typeset in Trixie plain.
The illustrations in this book
were rendered in mixed media.
Printed in Hong Kong.
ISBN 0-8118-2327-X

Library of Congress Cataloging-in-Publication Data
McCauley, Adam.
My friend Chicken / by Adam McCauley.
p.   cm.
Summary: Worried about the whereabouts of her absent
friend Chicken, a girl claims that she will not be distracted
by roaring rockets, dancing giraffes, or rollercoasters.
ISBN 0-8118-2327-X
1. Chickens—Fiction. 2. Friendship—Fiction. 3. Imagination—Fiction.
I. Title.
PZ7.M47841354My   1999
E —dc21   98-36187
CIP
AC

Distributed in Canada by Raincoast Books
8680 Cambie Street, Vancouver, British Columbia V6P 6M9

10 9 8 7 6 5 4 3 2 1

Chronicle Books
85 Second Street, San Francisco, California 94105
www.chroniclebooks.com

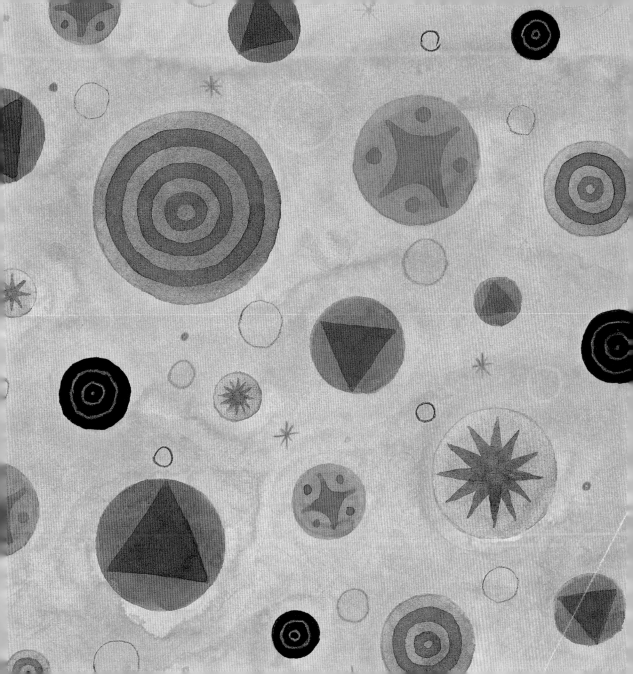

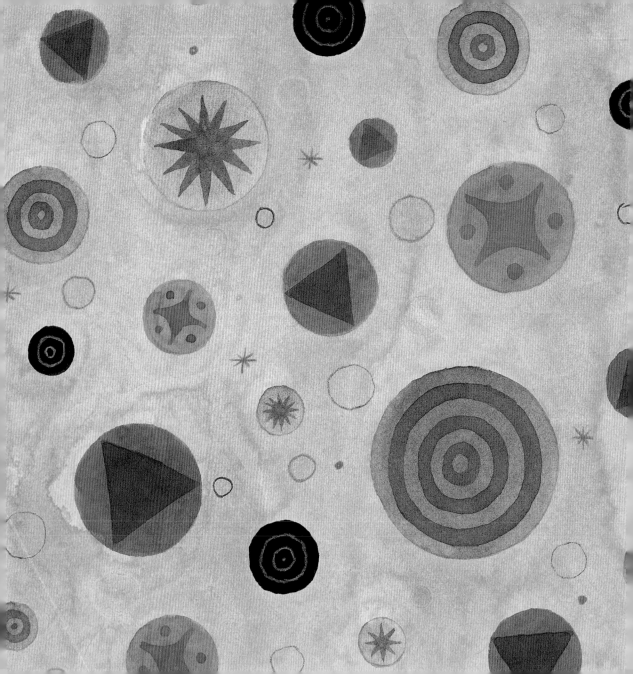